My Fruit, My Season!

Patsy Long

ISBN 979-8-88943-158-9 (paperback)
ISBN 979-8-88943-161-9 (hardcover)
ISBN 979-8-88943-159-6 (digital)

Christian Faith Publishing
832 Park Avenue
Meadville, PA 16335
www.christianfaithpublishing.com

All scriptures were taken from the King James version of the Holy Bible by Holman Bible Publishers.

The stories in this book are a work of fiction. Names, characters, places, and incidents are a product of my imagination. Any resemblance to actual persons is coincidental with the exception of "The World Is an Audience." The episodes of abuse and the occurrences of miracles are factual; however, the names, times, and locations have been changed. The story ending is fictional.

All poems and illustrations are my own. I began this work in 1988 as led by the Holy Spirit. It is now completed thirty-four years later.

Printed in the United States of America

I dedicate this book to my Lord and Savior, Jesus Christ, who inspires me every day and loves me despite my faults.

To my grandmother and my mother, who instilled in me the Word of God. Both were women of great faith.

To my beautiful daughter, Catrina; my granddaughter, Shelia; and my grandson, Eric.

> Then Peter said; Silver and gold have I
> none; but such as I have give I thee. (Acts 3:6)

This book is also dedicated to my eldest brother, Joseph, who gave his life for our country, and to my eldest sister, Francine, who was my mentor.

Everyone should have a special person in their lives who encourages them to always do their best. Someone who will listen and give them that little push when they feel like giving up. Someone whose arms will hold them when they need a hug and tell them that everything will be all right. I am blessed to have that special person in my life.

Tony Roberts, thank you. I appreciate you.

Love always,
Patsy

Contents

Preface

The purpose of this book is to uplift, encourage, give hope, enlighten, and send a positive message to all readers.

Between the covers, I will share bits and pieces of my life, from birth to joy and the journey in between, through poems, short stories, and songs.

I will also share the outcome of lessons I had to learn concerning the dangers of trying to make it on my own without seeking God first. I had to grow spiritually to realize that it is true that only what we do for Christ will last.

This is a book about love, and God is love.

Blessed Are the Righteous

Blessed is the man that walketh not
    in the counsel of the ungodly,
    nor standeth in the way of sinners,
    nor sitteth in the seat of the scornful.
But his delight is in the law of the lord;
    and in his law doth he meditate
    day and night.
And he shall be like a tree
    planted by the rivers of water,
    that bringeth forth his fruit in his season;
    his leaf also shall not wither;
    and whatsoever he doeth shall prosper.
The ungodly are not so:
    but are like the chaff
    which the wind driveth away.
Therefore, the ungodly shall not
    stand in the judgment,

nor sinners in the congregation
   of the righteous.
For the Lord knoweth the way
   of the righteous:
   but the way of the ungodly shall perish.

—Psalm 1

Season 1

Fruit of the Spirit

But the fruit of the spirit is love, joy, peace, longsuffering, gentleness, goodness, faith, Meekness, temperance: against such is no law.

—Galatians 5:22–23

A Warm Thought

Good morning! 'Tis the beginning of a brand-new day.
    The morning mist has disappeared; the sun is out to stay.

Magically, the dew appears as diamonds in the grass.
    The sun has turned the lake into a giant looking glass.

The flowers perfume the air; their scent is carried by the breeze.
    And very soon their nectar will be sampled by the bees.

Butterflies are playing tag across the fields of clover.
    Go out, enjoy the excellence before this day is over.

A Rainy Day

Shush! Listen! Falling rain, soothing, calming to the earth,
    Filling, quenching, satisfying, stimulating birth.
Slow down and rest, relax, enjoy, rejoice, reflect, release,
    Use this time to clear your mind, sit back and bask in peace.

Take a trip within your mind, on a stressless thoroughfare,
    Get lost in the beauty of your ride as you vacate to nowhere,
And when floodwaters take control and wash debris away,
    Suddenly, you'll feel inspired and thank God for a rainy day.

Such as Life

Perfect
    Pampered
Cradled
    Nourished
Adored.
Precious,
    Sheltered,

Confused
    Criticized
Pressured
    Disobedient
Bored.
Misunderstood,
    Unpredictable,

Responsible
    Loyal
Reliable
    Unappreciated
Stressed.
Dependable,
    Conscientious,

Prayerful
    Wise
Peaceful
    Joyful
Blessed.
Satisfied,
    Thankful,

Love

God has shown his LOVE for us throughout many generations,
His LOVE will endure forever and has no limitations.
Everyone that loves God must also LOVE his brother,
It is God's desire that we all LOVE one another.
Our LOVE is made perfect by he who dwells within,
Perfect LOVE will cast out fear and lead us out of sin.

LOVE is universal, unconditional, color-blind,
LOVE can be everywhere at the same time.
LOVE will see the beauty in every living thing,
And change a stony heart to one of understanding.

The romantic side of LOVE was woven into God's plan,
When he created woman and presented her to man.
Each to LOVE, honor, cherish, to have and to hold,
Thus, the beauty of oneness began to unfold.

LOVE speaks from the heart and is always near,
A loving heart is generous, sensitive, sincere.
Every day's a good day to reach out and LOVE someone,
God expressed it best when he gave his only Son.

Chest of Treasures

Precious is the joy you've brought to me,
    Priceless is your truth, your honesty,
Splendid are the pleasures that we share,
    Tender is the way you always care.

Pleasing is the smile upon your face,
    Trusting is the grip of your embrace,
Excellent is the substance of your love,
    Continually, it's you I'm thinking of.

Thoughtfully, you've helped me through rough times,
    Forever you're the subject of my rhymes,
To my words you gave a melody,
    You're a lifelong chest of treasures to me.

My Chocolate Fantasy

Here he comes again,
    To pick, to tease, to flirt with my heart.
I feel him staring,
    And he knows that I feel his eyes examining me,
As though I was a piece of art.

Right now in this moment,
    I feel beautiful, young and remember myself as I used to be.
And then he laughs,
    And the moment is gone, and I feel foolish,
For he is younger than me.

He's tall, brown, roguishly handsome,
    With an upper body that would make every woman scream.
Little does he know,
    Ten years ago, I could have been his dream.

At least now I know,
    That when the right man comes along, my body can still respond,
To the excitement of ecstasy.
    Thank you, my young, handsome, chocolate fantasy.

Is It Really You?

Are your arms the arms that I can get lost in and separate myself from the problems of the world,

Are your eyes the eyes that when focused on mine, I get to see the light of love beaming from your heart,

Are your shoulders the shoulders upon which I may lay my head when my mind simply wants to relax,

Are your lips the lips that will ignite the passion within me when you kiss me,

Are your hands the hands that will caress away my fears,

Is your love the complete love that only comes through Jesus,

The love I have been praying for all these years,

Love, is it really you?

A Perfect Place

Sixty-something years ago, I was a child of nine,
    I grew up in a perfect world that I would one day leave behind.
A world where we had neighbors who took the time to care,
    A world where you could park your car, come back, and find it there.

A world where I could go to school to learn and make new friends,
    Without the fearful thought of my life coming to an end.
I would go to church on Sunday and wear my Sunday shoes,
    And not worry that my pastor might rape me in the pews.

I used to go to playgrounds and climb the monkey bars,
    Without the scary thought of bullets fired from a car.
Looking back, I now realize there is no perfect place,
    There was a riot going on, the problem then was race.

That problem still exists today; when will people understand,
    The way to conquer hate is love towards our fellow man.

Mothers and Fathers

Mothers and fathers who are obedient to God, who are grounded in his word,
    And do not spare the chastening rod,
Create a legacy of wisdom that their children may be wise,
    For everything they teach them will affect them all of their lives.
As we shape our children's values, we shape the future of the world,
    We must be the examples to our boys and to our girls,
God has set the standard; we need only to adhere,
    It is our charge to raise them, not their sitters or their peers.

Feeding them the word of God will nourish their souls, give life to their spirits,
    And give wisdom more precious than gold,
That they may be wise unto salvation, through faith in Jesus Christ,
    The one who died on Calvary, the one who paid the price.

And when we have to leave them, they will understand that they are not forsaken,
    They've been placed in perfect hands,
The mighty hands of our Father, the hands that made us all,
    The hands that we held on to when we thought that we might fall.

Mothers and fathers are pleasing in God's sight, when yielding to his will,
    And walking in his light,
Both were made in God's own image, both created to honor him,
    And to teach and share his love with many generations of children.

A Message to My Father

Just a little note to let you know that I think of you often,
    'Til this day I still wonder if I've ever crossed your mind,
Do you think of the child you left behind?
    If you don't, it's okay, I don't hold against you your decisions of
    yesterday.
You were very young then, many years have gone by.
    Just know I have forgiven you, I no longer cry.

It would have been nice to have met the man I can't forget,
    I had all this extra love in me that should have gone to you,
I equally divided it among family, friends, and some strangers too.
    Just when I thought I had given all of your share away, a voice
    from deep within my heart,
    Told me what I needed to say.

It's hard to feel complete when a part of you is missing,
    This note was not written to make you feel sad or bad,
It was written to let you know that there will always be a vacancy
In my heart reserved for you, Dad.

Masterpiece

LOOK AT ME!
You won't see a trace of what I used to be
    when you first came along.

UNDERSTAND!
The person you are looking at is much different now
    because the love has gone.

CONGRATULATE YOURSELF!
You created this work of art,
    this cold statue with a matching heart.

REMEMBER THIS!
You can no longer hurt me because I no longer care,
    that hold you once had on my heart has vanished in thin air.

THINK!
Of how your master plan almost destroyed me,
    and when you're locked away in living hell, I'll be holding the
    master key.

In Memoriam

The year was 1968, a young man went to war,
    I was the last to see his face as he walked out the door,
He was his mother's eldest child, death had claimed her spouse,
    The young lad had big shoes to fill, when dubbed man of the house.

Respected by his siblings, admired by his friends,
    Coworkers called him special, they saw the light within,
That young man was my brother, he was the chosen one,
    He led us out of poverty at only twenty-one.

An angry bullet pierced his throat,
    It claimed my brother's life,
I know he's in a better place,
    Where there is no war, no hate, no strife.

A World in Despair

I see a world in great despair, reaching heights of disrepair,
Hopelessness, lawlessness, disrespect, greed, hunger, and much
neglect,
Lying tongues spewing seeds of hatred, brainwashed minds ignite a
takeover,
I see a world where love is void and in dire need of a spiritual
makeover.

Locked out, locked down, where is the joy, deployed camouflage like
carpet spread on the floor,
Covering alcoves and corridors, I think they call this war,
Angry bullets piercing skin, ending lives for no good reason, no
declaration of
Independence, but a declaration of hunting season.

Knees that have become weapons that kill seem to have approval up
on Capitol Hill,
It's as though the world is on a downward slope, it's time to cry
out to Jesus,
He is our saving hope.

As I Look Around

As I look around, I see turmoil and strife, men firing guns with no regard for life,
> Hatred, rioting, fighting, shooting, boarded buildings due to no-shame looting,

Poverty, filth, piled-up trash, blown-up ATMs minus the cash,
> Hundreds of people waiting in food lines, unemployment checks are months behind.

Thousands of people are dying daily, vaccination efforts surely failing,
> Masks are the fashion for the epidemic, schools are closed, so much for academics,

Churches are filled with empty pews while members are home praying for some good news.

Businesses forced to close their doors, outdoor dining above concrete floors,
> Our president must honor the oath he took, he has a mess to clean up behind the

Outgoing crook.
> I look around again, no good thing in sight, and then I looked upward towards

The marvelous light,
> At that very moment, I felt joy in my soul, I was reminded that God is still in control!

If These Legs Could Talk

If these legs could talk, they would tell you about the day I took my first steps that gave me my first taste of freedom.

No longer a need to be carried around, wheeled around, pushed around, or put down.

They would go on to tell you how they began to run one day, faster and faster, often without direction, protection, lacking perfection, in need of correction.

They would not forget to mention a twenty-minute walk to and from grammar school followed by a two-mile hike to and from high school.

Later mastering a life or death run through neighborhoods that did not accept people of color, leading to numerous fights because of dislikes that led to protest marches for civil rights.

Marches to eradicate injustices of racism, segregation, demanding equality and standing steadfast with determination in a struggle that would one day benefit all.

Yes, these legs were there, standing firm, standing proud, standing tall.

Season 2

Wisdom

My fruit is better than gold, yea, than fine gold; and my revenue than fine silver

—Proverbs 8:19

Wisdom

Wisdom is the ability to make good use of all we've learned,
    To distinguish right from wrong with the power to discern.
God is the source of wisdom that brings lasting satisfaction,
    It channels our feelings and controls our reactions.

Security and peace are the fruit of the wise,
    Who are lights that shine brightly and lead other souls to Christ.
The steps towards wisdom are reverencing the Lord,
    Seeking his kingdom, and trusting in his Word.

We should all ask him for wisdom to know what we are to do,
    And then ask for strength and courage to follow his plan through.
God's wisdom is available to all upon request,
    Once you have received it, you must put it to the test.
Apply it to your daily lives, walk by faith in love,
    The treasures of wisdom are hidden in Christ.
Hold fast to this gift from above.

Encourage

When you say unkind words,
　They hide the best of you.
They hide the love within your heart,
　And cancel the good you do.

When you do a good deed,
　Continue on that path.
For one day you may need a friend,
　To act on your behalf.

Don't ridicule and criticize,
　Instead, encourage with love.
You may be entertaining angels,
　On a mission from above.

Remember

It's sometimes hard to be yourself,
   Because some folks won't let you,
Even when you do your best,
   There are people out to get you.

But never let them take you down,
   To where they want to be,
Look to the hills and keep your faith,
   And you'll have the victory.

Think About This

Oftentimes we think we know when maybe we should listen,
Oftentimes we search to find that something that is missing,
The more we get, the more we want, we're never satisfied,
All of the things we really need have already been supplied.

No Cost Giving

It doesn't cost a penny to show someone you care,
 to let them know when chips are down, that you'll always
 be there.

It doesn't cost a penny to spend time with a friend,
 or visit one who is lonely or someone on the mend.

It doesn't cost a penny to sometimes share a meal,
 with someone who is hungry, think how much better they
 will feel.

It doesn't cost a penny to care and share and love,
 and in return you shall receive blessings from above.

True Words

As long as there's a song to sing,
There will always be a voice.
As long as there's a God above,
We'll always have a choice.

As long as there's an ear to hear,
God's Word shall be received.
Eternal life's an inheritance,
To all those who believe.

Rules to Live By

Appreciate the simple things in life.
Always be mindful of others.
Pray every day.
Remember to say thank you.
Love those who call themselves your enemies.
Ignore negativity.
Accept each new day as a gift and be thankful.
Initiate forgiveness.
Never allow anger to block your blessings.
Give as often as you can.
Let your light shine!

Driving Lessons

The roads of life are easier once you've learned the way,
  The quick shortcuts have oftentimes caused us to go astray.
Some bumps are caused by ignorance, disobedience, and pride,
  Sometimes the words "I'm sorry" will smooth a bumpy ride.

Some roads are full of potholes, which cause us to stop and go,
  Their purpose is to build our faith, they are there to help us grow.
Sometimes we're in the wrong lane and cannot make our turn,
  Once recognized, our big mistakes become a lesson learned.

Nighttime is approaching, fear not, do not despair,
  There is a light to guide you, he'll lead you safely there.

Young Girls Beware

The old man standing on the corner,
　Watching girls go by,
He smiles, he speaks, he compliments,
　But lust is in his eyes.

Beware of guys who work in pairs,
　They always want to share,
Just when you're alone with one,
　His friend pops up out of nowhere.

Stay away from married men,
　Who try to charm and woo you,
For when they get caught by their wives,
　They'll swear they never knew you!

There Is Still Time

If you knew you had one week to live, how would you spend those days,
Would you live them to the fullest, or let them waste away,
Would you forget about the bad things that happened in your life,
Or hold on to the bitterness the anger and the strife.

Could you let go of old hurt feelings and make the first move towards amends,
Or continue to dwell in stubbornness as your week comes to an end,
Would you spread the love that you have left, as far as it would go,
Or keep it locked inside yourself, afraid to let it grow.

A week is not a long time, you can overcome your fears,
Now is the time to make things right and gain eternal years.

Sugar Button

My name is Junias Timothy Begler, named after my grandfather. I am twelve years old and the youngest of three children. I have twin sisters, Deanna and Deidra. We live in a nice house with a big yard and have a dog named Jiggy. My dad is a dentist, and my mom is a social worker. I guess you think the story sounds normal so far. I don't like to complain because my grandmother always says we're blessed and should thank the Lord every day. However, I have a problem, and my grandmother is the source of my problem.

My sisters and I used to spend our summers at our grandparents' house. They had a lot of land where we could run and play. They had peach trees and a vegetable garden. They taught us how to pick butter beans and tomatoes. We loved being there. Three years ago, Pop-pop passed away, and Grandma was all alone in that big house. My mom and dad suggested she sell the house and move in with us, and that's what she did.

Grandma is so cool. She loves to bake cakes and cookies. She makes homemade ice cream, loves to hug and tickle us until we cry from laughing too hard. She tells funny jokes and even plays ball with me. She's the best. We say our prayers together. Grandma says that prayer is very important and it keeps us connected to God and to each other. She loves to read the Bible and teaches us that we can do all things through Christ who strengthens us (Philippians 4:13). My mom says we should all spend time talking with her because she enjoys sharing her wisdom and knowledge with us. "So what's the problem?" you ask. The problem is my nickname.

When my sisters and I were born, of course our parents named us. They thought it would be nice to let our grandparents choose our nicknames. They did okay with my sisters. Deanna would be called Annie, and Deidre would be called Dee-Dee, but when I was born, my grandmother took one look at me and said Sugar Button. Can you believe that? I'm the only boy, her first grandson, and she nick-named me Sugar Button.

I didn't mind when I was little, but now I am twelve years old. Sometimes she'll shorten it and call me Buttons, but that's just as bad. It's one thing to call me that in private, but to go outside and yell, "Sugar Button, it's dinnertime!" It does not stop there. When we're in church, the ladies pinch my cheeks and call me Buttons. The worst part is that one of my classmates, a girl, goes to my church, and she went back to school and told everybody—well, it seemed like everybody when they were teasing me.

There were so many other nice nicknames she could have cho-sen within my own name, JT, JB, Timmy. If I were a girl, it probably wouldn't have bothered me as much. This is now a real problem for me. Grandma always told me if I ever had a problem about anything, I could come to her and talk about it. So that's what I did.

One evening after dessert, I explained to her how I felt and how I was being teased at school because of my nickname. She hugged me, apologized, and said she agreed with me. She admitted I had outgrown that name and promised she would never call me Sugar Button again.

When we have problems, it's okay to go to our parents and grandparents and talk them through; problems can be solved.

That night, after we had said our prayers and everyone had gone to bed, Grandma came into my room, kissed me on my cheek, and said, "Good night, Junias. I love you."

"I love you too, Grandma."

The Children's Prayer

Our Father, which art in heaven, please help us to be all that you
want us to be,
    Our Father, which art in heaven, please help us to see, all that you
    want us to see,
We are sheep who need a shepherd, to guide us on our way,
    Give us a light that we may shine in our travels every day,
In the name of Jesus, these things we pray.

Our Father, which art in heaven, please help us to grow, as you would
have us to grow,
    Our Father, which art in heaven, please help us to know, all that
    you want us to know,
Build our faith and understanding, and knowledge of your Word,
    Build our thoughts to do your will through the teachings that
    we've heard,
In the name of Jesus, these things we pray.

Our Father, in heaven, we thank you each day, you gave your Son
Jesus to teach us the way,
In the name of Jesus, these things we pray.

Amen.

Season 3

Issues of the Heart

Introduction

This portion of the book addresses the struggles of four women and how they overcame their personal tragedies, heartaches, and disappointments by setting their affections on things above.

I was inspired by God to write these stories to give hope to all. Writing was and still is a source of healing for me. I was encouraged by a speech delivered by Dr. Martin Luther King regarding a man who had become distraught after losing the woman he loved.

The man wrote a song about her, and it became a huge hit. It was titled "Goodnight Irene." After hearing that speech, I began to keep a daily journal of my feelings, good and bad, and I thank God and praise him for giving me the strength I needed to make it through each day. The more I praised him, the more my hurt and pain turned into unspeakable joy.

I prayed my way through an abusive relationship. Prayer does change things and God can change hearts. Sometimes we have to stop trying to fix things on our own, step back, and let God have his way. He knows what is best for us, and he specializes in everything!

In time, my abuser and I became very good friends. He passed away but not before receiving Christ as his Lord and Savior. God worked it out for me, and I am so grateful.

I love writing about God's goodness, his mercy, and his grace. These short stories involve issues of the heart. I hope they are encouraging.

The Lord is my strength and my shield; my heart trusted him, and I am helped: therefore my heart greatly rejoiceth; and with my song will I praise him.

—Psalm 28:7

Lilian Owens

I am seventy years old and have been in church my entire life. I was raised by a praying grandmother who loved the Lord. She always encouraged me to read the Bible and made certain I attended Sunday school, Bible study, and vacation Bible school. And back then, there were buses that would come into the neighborhoods, transporting teachers who held Bible classes for the youth, and of course, she made sure I was on it. I was in church no less than four times a week. In my mind, I questioned her motives. I wanted to know why all that church was necessary.

As I look back, I can understand it now. Through her own life experiences and her love for God, she had received wisdom to know that I would need to know him for myself later down the road. She was so right, and I thank her for instilling in me the Word of God. She knew one day I would have to draw from his strength.

I married fresh out of high school. My husband enlisted in the Marines, and a few months later, we discovered I was pregnant. He was granted leave to come home to share the birth of our beautiful baby girl. So much had happened to us in a short period. I was only nineteen, and he was twenty-one. We could never have guessed that he would never see his twenty-second birthday as he left for Vietnam.

I had just come home from picking up my daughter from the babysitter after a rough day at work. I was just about to feed her when the doorbell rang. I opened the door, and there stood before me two men in uniform. I was overcome with a whirlwind of emotions. I was afraid, confused, defiant, and not in the mood for bad news, and I was thinking, "Please don't say it." But they said it anyway. Those awful words, "We regret to inform you." My mind went blank and my ears shut. It took a few minutes for me to comprehend the last part of that sentence. My husband, the man I loved, my best friend, and the father of my daughter had been killed by enemy fire in Quảng Nam, Vietnam. And to add insult to injury, I received a telegram confirming his death hours later. I was angry.

The days that followed were blurred. The Marine officers were very kind and handled all the arrangements. They also assigned two escorts to visit me throughout the two-week period until my husband's body arrived in the States. After the funeral, they stayed in touch for about a month. It was all so surreal. I was in mourning and still grieving, but God was with me. It was as though he went through it for me. It was like I was there but I wasn't there. I know it sounds strange, but God eased me through it. I just remember praying and asking him for help and strength, and he delivered. All I could do was lift my hands and praise him. I remembered a scripture quoted by my grandmother on many occasions: "Weeping may endure for a night, but joy cometh in the morning" (Psalm 30:5). I thank God for unspeakable joy!

Many years later, my daughter married, and she and her husband blessed me with three grandchildren, two girls and a boy. Sadly, her marriage didn't last; her husband abandoned her and the children. She got through it, continued to work as a nurse, bought a home for her family, and all was well. One evening, I was visiting a friend and I received a frantic call from my eldest granddaughter. She said she and her siblings had come in from playing and found my daughter facedown on the kitchen floor, so she called 911 and they were on the way. The ambulance and I arrived at the house at the same time. They turned her over and tried to resuscitate her. Helplessly I stood back as they lifted her on to the gurney and into the ambulance. The children and I followed the ambulance to the hospital, praying for good news.

Unfortunately, my daughter passed away. She died from a heart attack. I never knew she had a heart problem but later found out that she knew and didn't tell me because she didn't want me to worry. When the doctors gave me the news that she had died, it felt like something sharp had cut a hole in my soul and my heart, and everything inside me was caving in and falling down into that hole that had no bottom. That was the weakest moment in my entire life. My knees gave way, and I slumped to the floor like a wet rag. I was so far down in spirit and overcome with grief that all I could do was look up and call on God. That was the right thing to do, because you see, as I was looking up toward him, he was looking directly at me, and I felt his love as his mercy and his grace began to fall upon me like rain. Once again, he brought me through. He was with me every step of the way. He helped me face my new reality, a grandmother raising three young children. I remembered another scripture that my grandmother often quoted.

> And He said unto me, my grace is sufficient
> for thee; for my strength is made perfect in weak-
> ness. (2 Corinthians 12:9)

And that was twenty years ago. My grandchildren are doing fine. My eldest grand is a nurse, my grandson is an accountant, and my youngest is a beautician. They are a blessing to me, and they all look like their mother. God has been good to us. Through it all, he gives you a song. I am going to run on and Jesus is my running mate.

That is my story, and this is my song: "Running Mate."

Running Mate

First thing every morning, I thank him for the light,
My precious Lord protected me, he watched me through the night.
I put all my trust in Jesus, he'll guide me on my way,
And he'll lead me into heaven someday.

When I feel my problems are too much for me to face,
I can't waste my time worrying, I'm trying to run this race,
I pray in the name of Jesus, and he'll take it from there,
My Lord won't give me more than I can bear.

I'm running with Jesus, he's my running mate,
He's the one you've got to know to get inside the gate,
I'm running with Jesus, he's my guarantee,
And I thank the Lord for all he's done for me.

Kenya Tyree

I am a seventeen-year-old high school senior and daughter of a saved father, Kenneth Tyree, and a worldly mother, who walked away from her marriage and me seven years ago when I was ten. My father and I were devastated by her sudden desire to just pack up and leave. What drove her away?

In the years that followed, I would learn the lessons of forgiveness because none of us is perfect and we have all fallen short.

I have the best father in the world. I realize these past seven years haven't been easy for him, having to raise a teenage daughter. He is a God-fearing, hardworking, kind man, and he's funny. My dad loves old cars; buying and restoring them is his hobby. My aunt says he missed his calling and should design his own car. He equates everything to cars, for example, the church. He calls it a full-service station, where you can get filled up, tuned up, and get a "will" alignment, and all work is protected by a lifetime guarantee through Jesus. It doesn't stop there. When he decided to tell me about the "birds and the bees," he told me to get in the car, and he drove me to the Auto Mall. He walked me around the lot and pointed out all the brand-new, untouched, shiny cars and then asked the question, "Do you know that as soon as a man puts his key in the ignition and drives the car off the lot, it depreciates in value?" I told him not to worry. He taught me well, and I had no plans to be driven off the parking lot any time soon. I understood that he wanted me to remain shiny, new, and untouched.

After my mom left, I was surrounded by family who loved me. We all attended church together, and I am so grateful to God for my aunts, who advised me as I faced the challenges of peer pressure. They had my back, and I could always confide in them. They knew I was harboring anger toward my mother and marked scriptures in

the Bible for me to read concerning forgiveness. The first one was in
the Gospel of Luke 6:37.

> Judge not, and ye shall not be judged, con-
> demn not, and ye shall not be condemned: for-
> give and ye shall be forgiven.

They taught me to remember that no one is perfect and we all
make mistakes according to Romans 3:23.

> For all have sinned, and come short of the
> glory of God.

These scriptures have helped me to realize that I love my
mother, and now my thoughts are focused on the good times we
shared before she left, and there were many. Sometimes I look into
my dad's eyes, and I can tell that he still loves her too. I often hear
him praying, asking God to watch over her and keep her safe. My
prayer is that someday, she will come back home to us, and if she
doesn't, I understand that it is all according to God's will.

Most of my friends know that my mother left my dad and me,
and they seem to think that I am deprived because I don't talk like
them or dress like them and I refuse to make out with boys. I had to
explain to my best girl friend that I am an English major and there
are many words in my vocabulary that I can use to express myself
instead of curse words. Concerning the way I dress, I dress for comfort; outside of my school uniform, a pair of jeans and a T-shirt work
for me. I don't like midriff tops, low-rise peekaboo skirts, or three-
inch heels that are hard to walk in. I asked her if she knew that tat-
toos were forbidden by God in the Old Testament (Leviticus 19:28)
because she had so many that you could read her arms and know all
her business. As for making out with boys, I had to let her know that
I am a child of the King, too good to be making out in the stairwell
of the fire exit at school or in the back seat of a car. I gave her a Bible
and told her to read the Song of Solomon so that she'll understand
why I am holding out. I want to experience love, marriage, and sex

in that order and from God's point of view. Then I told her I was going to pray for her, and that surprised her. She said she thought only old people prayed, and that surprised me. I pray every day, and one of my prayers is that God would bless me to live to see old age. Three of our classmates died last year; one was by hit-and-run, and the other two were shot on the way home from school. I encouraged her to pray. My dad and I pray for my mother every night. We have forgiven her. We love her and want her to know that God loves her too. I find more and more reasons to pray as I grow.

This is my song: "As I Grow."

As I Grow

Jesus, as I grow, light my path that I may see,
My affections are in heaven, and my faith is in thee,
As I grow, I will follow the map you left for me,
Roads of goodness, trails of love, all lead to victory.

As I grow, I am filled with your spirit,
I've been rooted and grounded in love,
As I grow, I am reaching towards heaven,
All that's perfect comes from above.

Sandra Larchwood

I love children. They are a gift from God to be loved and nurtured. Without them generations would cease and mankind would become extinct. They bring much joy with their energy and inquisitiveness. They are like little sponges, absorbing everything and completely trusting and depending on their parents for everything. That's what God our Father wants us to do—to trust and depend on him.

I knew early in life that I wanted to become a teacher, and I am blessed to have my dream job as a high school teacher. I am thirty-five years old and unmarried with the desire to start a family someday. When the time is right, I'll have children of my own, but in the meantime, I have eleven nieces and nephews to keep me busy. I am also a counselor for the youth attending the after-school program at my church.

I've been waiting a long time for Mr. Right. I was raised in the church and often wonder if my standards are too high. I have dated a few really nice guys. The problem is, when I bring Jesus into our conversation, they back away. One gentleman asked me if I was going to start preaching at the table, and that hurt my feelings. I just want a man who loves the Lord the way I do or at least has the desire to learn about him. There was one guy who tricked me into going out with him. He told me he went to church every Sunday. After we went out to dinner a few times, I told him I would love to visit his church, then took it a step further and invited him to my church—never happened. He always had an excuse. I later found out that he was telling the truth about going to church every Sunday. He was taking his mother. He would drop her off and go back later to pick her up. It seemed to me it would have been easier to stay, enjoy the service, and save himself a trip. I no longer dwell on it even though I realize my biological clock is running out. I have decided to leave it all in God's hands. He knows what's best for me.

In my line of work, I come in contact with children from all walks of life. I must tell you, it saddens me to see so many angry children. I personally believe that many of them simply need more positive people in their lives whom they can talk to. They are under a tremendous amount of pressure, much more than I had to deal with in my youth. Their role models are sports personalities and rap artists. They want the expensive sneakers and jackets. They look up to the rappers who became famous with their vulgar lyrics and loud and vulgar clothes to match. Of course, there are exceptions. Their best friends are cell phones and social media. How can we blame them when the people they once trusted betrayed them? Mothers and fathers using or selling drugs or both and, in some cases, selling to their own children; pastors and priests molesting children; teachers having sex with students; and I can't forget the gang situation where member initiation involves killing someone. Children today have to grow up too fast, and many of them are afraid. Afraid to walk to school, afraid to play outdoors, afraid to ride public transportation, afraid to walk to the corner stores. Gone are the days when as a child you could have fun playing jump rope, hopscotch, wall ball, dodgeball, marbles, jacks, hide-and-go-seek, and the list goes on. They have a strong fear of being killed by a stray bullet. So now they are indoors with violent video games and social media—such a tragedy. I wish parents could spend more time with their children, and I understand that many of them work and are tired when they get home. I would encourage all parents to pray with their children, take them to church, and when trying to buy everything on their birthday list or Christmas list, add on a Bible and read it with them even if only an hour a week. It teaches values, respect, and how to love and treat others.

About a year ago, one of my students asked if he could attend the after-school program at my church. Of course, I said yes. I'm always excited when they come willingly, wanting to better themselves. I think God gets excited also when we willingly seek him. The student's name is Ahmad Wilkes. He was seventeen at that time and had lost his mother to cancer two years prior to our meeting. He had been raised in the church, but neither he nor his father had attended since her passing.

Ahmad arrived early along with his father, who had driven him. I immediately introduced myself and welcomed them both. However, his father said he wasn't staying; he just wanted to check out the facility. I commended him for that, and he left. We began our discussion, and surprisingly, Ahmad was very forthcoming with information about himself. I didn't have to pull it out of him as I often had to do with many of the youth. He said he was angry with God for taking his mother away from him and his dad. He said he was also angry with himself for life-altering changes caused by poor decisions he had made. At only seventeen and in his senior year in high school, he had already fathered two babies and was contemplating dropping out of school to take on a full-time job. His part-time job at a fast-food restaurant wasn't paying enough, and the mothers of his children were on his back for financial support. I saw the sincerity in his eyes as he expressed to me his desire to be a good father. He felt he had messed up his life for good. I let him know that he had options and dropping out was not one of them. We all make mistakes in life, and that doesn't make us bad people. I told him not to worry because I was going to help figure all this out and my starting point would be to call a meeting with the parents and grandparents of the children. When we see our children trying, we must help them. I told him I expected great things from him because I could see he had a good heart and God sees the heart. I opened my desk drawer and reached in for a Bible, and I handed it to him along with scriptures of encouragement. As a teacher, I can't do that in my classrooms because it is not permitted.

The meeting I had arranged with the families ended with positive results. There were three families involved, and they all agreed this was a family matter and they had to do what was best for the children—Ahmad, the two young mothers, and the two babies. They agreed to help with the finances, allowing the three young parents to complete their high school education. After graduation, they would schedule online college courses that would not interfere with their work hours. Ahmad wanted to pursue a career in engineering, following in his father's footsteps, who had a position waiting for him once he completed his training. When I looked into Ahmad's eyes, I no longer saw the anger, only hope. He and his father thanked me and invited me to dinner. I accepted.

I encouraged Ahmad to go back to church, and he expressed to me that it was too hard for him and his father to go back and not see his mother ushering or singing on the choir. My next thought was to invite them to attend Sunday services at my church. As Ahmad prepared to leave our follow-up session, I invited him and his father to our Family and Friend's Day at my church. The following Sunday, I saw them walk in, and my heart almost burst with joy. They came every Sunday after that.

Months have passed since Ahmad's graduation, and all is going well for him. He and his dad have become closer, and things are cordial between the two mothers of his children. He stopped in to see and inform me that he wanted to be a blessing to someone else; he wanted to mentor youth in the after-school program. I told him that sometimes, God, through his permissive will, allows certain things to happen in our lives that will draw us closer to him because he loves us. He can fix us. We just need to trust him. He sent his Son Jesus to save us and his Holy Spirit to lead and guide us. He is gracious and full of compassion. I am so grateful for the call on my life to reach out to and teach the children and Ahmad, who are a blessing to me. I told him that mentoring would be great as long as he put aside time to continue to build his relationship with God. I said to him lovingly, "You need Jesus!" The truth of the matter is, we all need Jesus.

A couple of days later, his father invited me to dinner, just the two of us. God, did you set this up?

My story, my song: "You Need Jesus."

You Need Jesus

You need Jesus, you really ought to get to know Jesus,
He loves us, he'll fix us, he'll make us right.
You need Jesus, sit down and have a talk with Jesus,
He will light your path and give you new sight.

Know the peace of God, which surpasses all understanding,
Let the peace of God rule in your heart,
For the gift of God is eternal life through Jesus Christ our Lord,
If you believe in him, and trust in him, and follow him,
He'll change your whole life.

You need Jesus, you really ought to get to know Jesus,
He's available, and he's waiting for you.

Season 3

The World Is an Audience

Introduction

Just as there is beauty in poetry, beauty in dance and in the other arts, there is beauty in life. The way we live and the way we care and get along with others can be as beautiful as a magnificent painting on display, to be admired or to possibly inspire someone. For this reason, we must be careful in the way we speak and act, and also be aware that the world is an audience, and someone in that audience may be watching you. Allow them to see something beautiful. Beauty, just as love comes from within. God is love!

"My Father in heaven, I thank you for guiding me through this day, and I ask that you would watch over me through this night if it is your will. Please bless all my family and friends. For those who call themselves my enemies, Father, bless them, open their eyes, and give them new sight. As I pray for them, please open my heart to forgiveness and my mind to understanding. Lead me and guide me in all that I do. I know that I can do all things through Christ who strengthens me. Please keep me humble and have mercy upon me. Bless each and everyone, everywhere, every day. These things I ask in Jesus's name, amen."

This was the prayer of Mrs. Janice Morgan. It was her daily prayer for the world.

These words would carry her through hurt and pain caused by a marriage of physical abuse, strengthen her faith, and restore her joy as she enters a new life of love and peace. To God be the glory!

Chapter 1

My name is Janice Morgan. I am the youngest of five children. I was born into a world where resentment preceded my birth. My mother had become pregnant during a one-year separation from her husband. She had given me his last name, causing quite a stir among his family. They slandered her name, labeled her unfit, and immediately fought to have my four siblings taken away from her, but all attempts failed. They closed their eyes to his infidelity, having fathered a child, who is eight months older than I am, with another woman before the separation. Sadly though, he was killed accidentally by a girlfriend while playing with a gun in bed.

For the next few years, my mother struggled to raise all five of us alone. Every other weekend, her in-laws would pick up their grandchildren. They would bring them home on Sunday evenings, and I would watch as my siblings paraded around the house in their new clothes and flaunted their new toys. There was never a toy for me. They would spend every summer with their grandparents, and once again, it would be just the two of us, Mom and me. I always wondered why I couldn't go with them, but as I grew older, I learned that they were not my grandparents and they didn't want anything to do with me. I remember that as though it were yesterday because it hurt.

For a time, I was passed around my mother's family like a hand-me-down. I knew it was done to protect me from all the gossip. One year, I was sent to South Carolina to spend the summer with my aunt and cousin. It was okay, but I missed my mother and I let my feelings be known, so they returned me to my mother. My mother's eldest sister, who had no children, wanted me to stay with her and my uncle every other weekend. They were very nice to me, but I just wanted to be home with my mother. Why was that so hard for everyone to understand?

The world is an audience, and someone in the audience was watching, and she did not like what she saw. Her name was Ms. Anna Johns, who had been a friend of my maternal grandfather after his wife had passed away. She had become very close to my mother and wanted to help. She convinced my mother that she could give me a better life and shield me from the resentment I was receiving. Although I was a young child, I felt it and never forgot it. A decision was made against my wishes, and soon after, Ms. Anna became my legal guardian and would be referred to as my grandmother.

Chapter 2

It took a while for me to adjust, accept, and settle into my new home. I was an audience of one, watching her every move, waiting for her to slip up so that I could go back to live with my mother. What I discovered was a kind woman with a loving heart and a personal relationship with God. She was always visiting and taking food to sick friends and family members. She sat with me and explained that I would spend every summer with my mother and siblings; that made me happy. She also explained to me that even though my biological father was not present in my life, I would never be fatherless because I had a Father in heaven, who would always watch over me. I carry that knowledge with me till this day everywhere I go. I had other male figures and role models in my life, my grandfather, uncles, brothers, and cousins, so I never dwelled on the fact that my father was not in my life. You don't miss what you never had.

It was nice having my own room and bed. Gone were the days waking up soaked because someone had wet the bed or having someone's foot in your face. I loved mealtimes because we had meat every day, and I could have second helpings. Every morning and night, my grandmother and I said our prayers on our knees together. We attended church every Sunday. She taught Sunday school and sang on the senior choir, and I sang on the youth choir. She let me know up front that Sunday was the Lord's day, no cooking, no laundry, no ironing, no work. You had up until Saturday to do all that. She enrolled me into grammar school and gifted me a journal to record my thoughts and feelings. I think she guessed I had many. She was strict, but I knew it was for my own good. Four of her instructions still resonate with me: First, always speak with intelligence, no slang or profanity. Second, if someone hits you, hit them back because if they are big enough to give a lick, they are big enough to take one. Third, once you become employed, pay your tithes and pay your bills; pay yourself in that order. Lastly, she said God knows my needs and gave me the scripture, "But seek ye first the Kingdom of God and His righteousness and all these things shall be added unto you" (Matthew 6:33).

I landed a job immediately after graduating from high school. I helped support my mother and grandmother for the next two years. My mother remarried and moved to New Jersey. That summer, I found an apartment, and within eighteen months, I had married and given birth to a beautiful daughter, Danyel Janaye Morgan.

Chapter 3

I was now Mrs. Janice Morgan, married to David Morgan. I loved having a last name with no controversy attached to it, as was the case when I was born. I met David while working as a waitress. He was a regular customer who would often request a table at my station. He was handsome, charismatic, and he always left a generous tip. One night, he asked me to accompany him to an upcoming basketball game, and I said yes. During the ride home after the game, he told me he was a driver for a beer distributor, made good money, and owned a three-bedroom house. These were all pluses in my book, and he was driving a very nice car. He confessed to me that he was previously married and was now divorced. He had dated a former classmate and had unprotected sex. When she found out that she was pregnant, they decided that getting married was the proper thing to do. The marriage didn't work out, so they agreed to divorce. After the divorce, she moved away, and he had no knowledge of their whereabouts. He wanted to see his son and went to her family for information, but they would not give him any. Apparently, she did not want to be found. I expressed that I thought it was cruel that she would keep his son away from him. I had completely missed the first red flag! He also told me both of his parents were deceased and that he had a brother and sister, each living in walking distance from his house, and his cousin and her family and two children lived across the street from him. She and I would one day become best friends. Her name was Celeste.

I shared with him that I lived alone in an apartment building. I told him of the sheltered life I had lived with my grandmother, who raised me and the promise I had made to myself that as soon as the opportunity presented itself, I would get my own place, live under my rules, and handle my own life. Looking back, I realized I had been so anxious to do things my way that I forgot to seek God first before making some very bad decisions.

After three months of a whirlwind relationship, David asked me to move in with him, and I declined the offer. I explained to him that I would not live with a man who was not my husband. Two weeks later, he came with a ring and a proposal. I said yes! Our wedding nuptials were performed by the justice of the peace at City Hall as our four witnesses looked on. We chose not to have a reception, so my grandmother organized a dinner party for our closest family and friends. The following morning, we left for Montreal, Canada, for a week's stay at the Queen Elizabeth Hotel. I was so happy!

Chapter 4

The weeks that followed our honeymoon were beyond my wildest dreams. David introduced me to the world of travel. We visited many of the places I had dreamed about—Vegas, Disneyland, Mexico, and New Orleans. We joined a bowling league and partied in clubs. I felt like I was living in a whole new world. This was all new to me, and when we received the news from my doctor that I was pregnant, that was the frosting on the cake. I had no idea that all this happiness and excitement was about to come to an end.

Six months into our marriage, I began to wonder if I had made a terrible mistake. David had become very possessive, and I realized he had a bad temper and mood swings. I thought it strange I hadn't noticed this behavior while we were dating. The expression "Love is blind" came to my mind, and now I know it's true because I did not see any of this beforehand. I hoped things would get better after the birth of our baby.

I went out on maternity leave in my seventh month of pregnancy. I thought this would be the perfect time to get my driver's license. We had discussed getting a second car, and that would be great for me because I could drive the baby to my grandmother's, drop her off, and then drive to work rather than struggling with public transportation, especially since we worked different hours. That night, I brought up the subject at dinnertime and was in no way prepared for the response I received. He became so angry that his face turned red, and it appeared to me that he was swelling up. For a second, I thought maybe it was an allergic reaction, but then he began yelling. He stood up, and the words came out of his mouth like a dragon's fire. "I have always taken you everywhere you asked to go, so why do you need to drive? Is there some man you need to see?" Before I could answer, he put both his hands beneath the tabletop and turned the table over, spilling everything onto the floor. I stood dumbfounded in shock and disbelief as I watched him grab his cap and walk out the door. I heard him slam the car door and race off. Still in shock, I did what I always do in a crisis—I prayed. I asked God to protect him, calm his temper, and guide him home safely. I cleaned up the mess and went to bed. He came home the next morning to change his clothes for work. He apologized, I forgave him, but things would never be the same. I never mentioned driving again.

Celeste was a godsend. She would always call me whenever she went food shopping or to the malls. She was a member of the Eastern Stars, which was a branch of the Masonic Organization. Her husband was a Mason. They were always sponsoring and promoting special events. Celeste made certain I got out of the house because she knew David hardly ever took me anywhere anymore, and he only trusted me to go out with his family. I had a great time hanging out with her. There were casino trips, beef and beers, barn dances, and they held sessions at five-star hotels where you go from room to room eating and drinking while having good conversations with other branch members. She asked me if I wanted to join, and I declined because often they traveled out of state for conventions, and I knew David would never go for that. We became very close and were often mistaken for sisters. She was actually more of a sister to me than my blood sisters were.

Chapter 5

Our daughter was born in February, a week after my due date. She was beautiful, and David was a proud father. He had wanted a girl. My first two weeks of motherhood were rough. I was sore from stitches, and it was hard for me to sit. I had no one to help me as I healed. David didn't take any time off from work. I got through it and found joy during the three months at home with my baby. I had already spoken to my grandmother about babysitting, and she was so willing and excited. She could hardly wait.

The day had come for me to return to work. My day began at four in the morning. I had to cook breakfast and prepare lunch for David, who left at five for work. I then proceeded to get myself and Danyel ready in time to catch the 5:38 bus to my grandmother's, drop her off, and then run to catch the el so I could make it to work by seven. I had my hours changed to an earlier shift so that I could pick Danyel up and get home in time to have dinner ready for David. I had enrolled at Community College with the intention of attending class two nights a week to become a CPA; however, after two weeks I dropped out. It was too much for me. My classes were from eight to ten, and by the time I got home and studied, it was well past midnight before I went to bed.

We were once again a two-income household and had saved enough to get a new car. Rather than giving me the old car, David gave it to his sister. I never commented on it; all I did was think to myself, "Wow," as I continued to use public transportation. Our marriage seemed to be heading southward. He accused me of not showing him enough affection. I suggested as calmly as I could that if he would help and lessen my workload, I would have more time to be affectionate. I ran it down to him that all he did was go to work, hang out with his friends after work, come home, eat, grab a beer, watch TV, and go to bed. And then I ran down my schedule. I cook breakfast, pack his lunch, drop the baby off, go to work, pick the baby up, cook dinner, wash the dishes, iron his work clothes, clean the house, do the laundry, and I shop for groceries while he sits waiting in the car. His comeback was, "Why can't we spend Sundays together? Do you have to go to church every Sunday?" That was when I made my next mistake. My prayer life was already lacking. I would fall asleep on my knees while praying because I was tired, and now I had agreed to stop going to church to satisfy my husband, not thinking at the time that I was putting him before God. I explained my situation to my grandmother, and she suggested that I let Danyel stay with her from Friday night until Sunday evening. This way, David and I could spend quality time together.

Chapter 6

Our new weekend schedule seemed to be working well for us. David and I would dine out Friday and Saturday nights, getting in that quality time. I had received a promotion at work, along with a substantial raise, and things were really looking up. Our sex life had increased, and my grandmother loved having the extra time with Danny. I had no complaints. All was well for two months, and then things took a turn for the worst.

One of my coworkers had invited us to her birthday party on a Friday night. I had bought myself a new outfit and David a matching shirt, then picked up a card and gift. I had been looking forward to this event. It was early evening when I arrived home. I took my shower and did my nails. (Back in those days, women did their own nails.) I lay across the bed and fell asleep. When I awoke, it was nine and no David. Cell phones weren't in existence yet, so I couldn't call him directly. I called a few family members, but no one had seen or heard from him. All I could do was wait. He didn't come home that night.

He got in at six thirty in the morning. I was furious and upset, yet relieved that he was okay. I asked him where he had been all night, and he gave me the lame excuse that he had hung out with his friends, drank too much, and was unable to drive. So I asked him why he didn't call; he knew we were supposed to go to a party. He claimed he forgot about the party and didn't call because he didn't want to hear me fussing. Next, I asked him where he stayed, and that's when I saw him turn red and swell up. He gave me a backhand across my face and told me I wasn't his mother or his father and he didn't have to answer to me. I ran upstairs and looked into the bathroom mirror and saw that my face was swollen where he had hit me. I went back downstairs to get some ice, and he went upstairs, got in bed, and went to sleep. Neither one of us spoke the rest of that day.

Sunday morning, I looked in the mirror and saw that I had a black eye. I immediately called my grandmother and told her I was sick with a fever and asked her if it was okay if we didn't come to pick Danny up. Of course, she said it was fine. I always left extra clothes and supplies over there for her. When David finally got up and saw my face and eye, he apologized, made a fresh ice pack, and held it to my face as he held me.

That Monday morning, I went into work wearing sunglasses. No one asked me anything, and I was glad. The world is an audience, and I knew they had all drawn their own conclusions. That was one long day. It's hard sometimes to focus at work when you have so many thoughts running through your mind. When I arrived home, dinner was ready and the table was set. David apologized again, and I told him I had forgiven him, but what he didn't know was that another little piece of my heart had been chipped away. We had light conversation before going to bed. He held me, but I felt nothing.

By Wednesday, my eye was looking better. I was approached by Mr. Mullen, the maintenance man at work. He was a kind elderly man. He asked me how I was feeling. He said my morning smile always brightened his day and that he hadn't seen it lately. So I smiled and asked him if he felt better. He smiled back and let me know he would be there for me if I ever needed to talk. I had never shared any of my personal business with any of my coworkers. Apparently, Mr. Mullen had detected the unhappiness I constantly tried to hide. I began to open up to him. I talked about David, but not in a negative way. He encouraged me to read the Bible for in it I would find strength. And that's exactly what I did. I realized that I always prayed and grew up in the church, yet I had never really studied the Bible. They say that hindsight is twenty-twenty. Looking back, I now understand that once you commit to studying God's Word, the Bible will come alive and you will have ears to hear the words as they speak directly to you. You will develop a relationship with God, and his Spirit will lead and guide you. I began writing in my journal again. I wrote down all my thoughts and feelings. I began to write poems. Sometimes I would read them to Mr. Mullen. He said I had a talent for writing and gave me scriptures to read concerning talents

(Matthew 25:14–30). I read them and never forgot them. Growing up, my grandmother encouraged me to read, and I continued reading well into my adult life. It was my way of coping. I would read three or four books a week. I would get lost in them. Now I had made the decision to read the Bible, the book that gives me hope. I committed to reading at least five chapters every day. God's Word gave me peace.

Chapter 7

As the years breezed by, my marriage became a nightmare, a bad dream with no ending. One beautiful Sunday afternoon, David announced that he was going to play ball with his coworkers. They had formed a softball team. I didn't mind. I was happy to have the house all to myself. I poured myself a glass of lemonade, made my way into the living room, and had just settled down on the sofa to watch a movie when the doorbell rang. I looked through the blinds and saw a woman with a baby in her arms. I was thinking she probably had the wrong house as I opened the door. Instantly she asked, "Is David home?" And I replied, "No, he isn't." She went into her handbag and pulled out a long white envelope and handed it to me and said, "When he gets home, give this to him and tell him I mean fast."

"Okay" was all I could say. I watched her leave with the baby, and I stood frozen for a moment before I closed the door, clenching that long white envelope. I broke out in a cold sweat, and my heart felt like it was going to pump right out of my chest. My knees became weak as I was trying to make it to the sofa so I could sit down and sort things out. So many thoughts were running through my mind—in fact, too many. I remembered the time I thought I smelled perfume on him and about the crazy hours he spent after work, getting home late every night. We rarely had sex anymore, which was fine with me. There was one time, a baby picture fell out of his pocket as I was sorting clothing to be taken to the dry cleaners, and he explained it away by saying his friend had asked him to be godfather to his child and had given him the picture. Here lately, his portion of the bill money had been short, and I had to make up the slack. What a fool I had been, completely ignoring all the signs that had been there for me to see. I looked at that envelope one more time and knew I had to open it, so I did. Enclosed was a letter addressed to David.

> Dear Daddy, David, Mr. Morgan, or whatever you want me to call you,
>
> Those pampers you bought me when I was first born have run out. I have outgrown those little outfits you gave me. It takes money to supply me with the things I need, and my mommy doesn't have enough. If you don't volunteer to help her, I'm going to ask her to take you to court.
>
> Love,
> Your sweet little daughter

The letter had been written by the child's mother. I never realized there could be forty-eight hours in one afternoon. I sat motionless for hours while waiting for David to return home, which was a blessing because that time had allowed me to calm down. If he had come home immediately after that incident, I might have hurt him.

When he got in, I waited patiently while he changed his clothes, showered, came downstairs, and went to the refrigerator to get his beer before I handed him the letter. As he read the letter, I watched every emotion that crossed his face, anger to guilt to sorrow. Without him saying a word, I knew he had done everything and told every lie he could to keep the truth from me. He looked at me, apologized, and came toward me, and I stopped him cold. "Don't touch me! Don't you dare touch me," I said in a voice that neither I nor he had heard before, a voice that let him know that he had lost the best friend he ever had, the only woman he had ever trusted, and the only person he could depend on. I had given him my all, and he betrayed me. My all had been misplaced. Now as I look back over my life, I realize that I had been so busy trying to give my all to my job, receiving many perfect attendance awards, employee of the month awards, free tickets to events, giving my all to my daughter, running back and forth to school recitals and Saturday morning dance classes followed by music lessons, trying to give her a memorable childhood, unlike the one I had, and finally giving my all to an undeserving, cheating husband. I had stopped going to church because my husband wanted me to spend Sunday mornings with him when I should have been going to God's house to worship and give him praise and thanks for giving his only begotten Son, who gave his all for me.

Although David had messed up big time, he vowed to never let me go. He went out and bought a gun and threatened to kill me if I ever left him. He continued to hang out with his friends. He would get paid on Thursday, and I wouldn't see him until Sunday. He completely stopped paying bills. I was fine with all that. When he was away from home, it was peaceful, and I earned enough money to cover the bills. I let him do his thing. I started going back to church. Some Sunday mornings he would come just as I was about to leave for church and offer to take me, but shortly after I got in the car, he would start an argument. Those mornings I had to dry my tears before entering the sanctuary. I just kept on praying he wasn't going to stop me from going.

I had recently received information concerning his ex-wife. One of his family members informed me that she left him because she was secretly taking birth control pills and when he found out about it, he accused her of cheating on him and beat her up. That was the reason she left and took their son without leaving a forwarding address. He was abusive.

Chapter 8

I find it interesting how fast time passes by as we get older. It seemed as though I blinked twice and Danny was no longer my little girl. She had become a teenager who had outgrown her dolls and toys and set her affections on clothes, makeup, and money. She was an A student, which made me very proud. She loved to draw and dance, so of course, I encouraged those activities and supported her dream of becoming a professional dancer. I wish someone had asked me what my dreams were when I was growing up. In my family, the rule was that you finished school, got a job, and helped to support the family. That is what I did. Each report period, Danny and I would celebrate her good grades. We would take in a movie, get a bite to eat, and shop at her favorite store so she could pick out whatever she wanted. I knew she sensed that her dad and I were having problems even though I tried to keep them hidden. Every summer, she spent two weeks in New Jersey with my family. It was a better environment, and my mother had an in-ground pool installed and a basketball court. Mom had given birth to two more children by her second husband, and my siblings relocated from Philadelphia to be close to her. She loved having all eighteen of her grandchildren over, and they loved being there. There was one saying that my mother instilled in all of us: "Take God with you everywhere you go." I am so grateful that I was raised by two amazing, strong women of faith who put their trust in God.

David had become insanely jealous, accusing me of every man I came in contact with, including my doctor, my pastor, my boss, and even his own brother. He would dream about me cheating and wake me up in the middle of my best sleep to accuse me. He claimed his dreams didn't lie. When we were out together, I would pray we wouldn't run into any of my old schoolmates or coworkers because if they spoke to me, I would have to explain how, when, and where

I knew them from. My situation had become so bad I would almost have a panic attack if my buses or trains were late because that would be the one time he came home early and I would have to convince him that I was not seeing anyone. His guilty conscience was making him crazy.

One day, he asked me how I felt about having his daughter over to meet and spend time with Danny. I told him I had no problem with it. (I didn't tell him his request caused an old hurt to resurface. I was sick with the flu, on my birthday, years ago. I asked Celeste to take me to the hospital. David didn't come home that night. I later found out the reason was because he was at another hospital, with another woman, giving birth to a baby girl on my birthday.) Anyway, I didn't mind.

His daughter's name was Sandra; we called her Sandy. She stayed with us for a weekend. Danny loved having a younger sister, and they got along great together. We all did, the three of us. David had no time for her. I treated her as though she were my own. During the holidays and birthdays, I shopped for her gifts and put David's name on everything. I didn't want Danny or Sandy to know that their father no longer had interest in special occasions.

Sandy spent two weeks with us during the summer. I had taken two weeks' vacation. The second Monday of my vacation, I had prepared breakfast for the girls and was about to go upstairs when David came in from being out all weekend. Without even saying, "Good morning," he asked me for money. I told him I didn't have any money to give him and turned to go upstairs. He grabbed me from behind, pulled me to the floor, and punched me in my face while calling me names. Before I could recover, he was out the door. I looked up and saw two horrified, tear-streaked faces staring at me. Once again, an audience was watching. I got up, went to the phone, and called Sandy's mother to come pick her up. And I called my grandmother, and she sent a cab for Danny. Neither of them would stay in that house again. I had to make a plan. My marriage was over.

Chapter 9

Part 1

Another summer had passed, taking with it the beautiful butterflies, the carpets of green grass, the lilies of the field, and the bonus hours of sunlight, leaving behind empty beaches, withering flowers, gated storefronts, "Closed for the Summer" signs and fond memories.

Autumn was upon us. The colorful leaves were vying for attention before they fell upon the earth, dried up, and swished beneath our feet. They filled our nostrils with the fragrance of the season. It was a beautiful season, yet sad, because we knew that shortly, the tree limbs would become naked and exposed. This summed up my marriage. The sunlight had turned into darkness, the love was beginning to wither away, and everything was about to be exposed, leaving me with memories of a failed marriage.

Part 2

It was a warm afternoon in late October. I didn't feel like going straight home from work. I decided to go shoe shopping with one of my coworkers. I arrived home a little after five thirty. It wasn't late, but it was dark. I hadn't left a light on in the house. I put my key in the door, unlocked it, opened it, reached for the light switch, and was punched in my mouth so hard that my teeth cut through my bottom lip. It was David. He grabbed me, pulled me to the sofa, pushed me down, ripped off my pants, (my favorite pair), pulled down my panties, spread my legs, and pressed down on my stomach, expecting to see semen running out of me. I asked him if he had found what he was looking for. I immediately began explaining that I had gone shopping. I told him to search my bags that I had dropped onto the floor along with my purse as I was being attacked. The one time I came home late, he decided to come home early. He had parked where I wouldn't see the car and waited in the dark for me to come home. How sick was that? He left me alone and went upstairs. I was so angry and frustrated. I collected my things and my thoughts as I went upstairs to look at my mouth. I could taste the blood. I walked into the bathroom, wet a washcloth with cold water, and applied it to my mouth and lip. I then entered the bedroom and couldn't believe what I saw. There he was on the bed naked, waiting for me to have sex. I accommodated him. I dared not refuse him.

Afterward, he complained that I was dry. I thought to myself, "Being punched in the mouth is not a turn-on for me," but said nothing while praying silently.

Part 3

The following week, I found myself questioning my behavior. Why was I putting up with his crap? He wasn't doing anything for me. I was paying all the bills, including the mortgage and my name was not on it. I handled all the repairs, bought all the food, and every time I stepped into the car, I had to put gas in it. I'd always considered myself to be intellectually astute and quick-witted. I'd never allowed anyone to hit me without hitting back. My grandmother taught me that. I had always spoken up for myself and others. I had been a union representative at one time. I took care of myself and my daughter even though she was staying with my grandmother temporarily. Then it dawned on me; I had loved this man and I honored my vows. I couldn't deliberately hurt someone that I loved. He didn't deserve me! I began praying for him more than my situation. I prayed that God would change his heart and open his eyes. I had lost my joy while trying to be a good wife. I had never cheated on him.

Part 4

Two weeks later, at about five in the morning, the phone rang. I was in the bathroom, and David answered the phone. He called me and said that it was for me. I hurried to answer, thinking it was some sort of emergency. When I answered, it turned out to be a wrong number; they asked for someone else. I asked David why he called me to the phone when the person didn't ask for me. He said that was my man and he had used a fake name because he had answered instead of me. I was furious, and I told him how ridiculous he was, and I watched him reach for something in the closet. He pulled out a gun and pointed it toward me. I was scared to death. He then told me he wanted to see how my brains would look splattered on the wall. I fell to my knees begging him to think about what he was about to do. I was crawling on the floor pleading for my life, trying to convince him that he was wrong. I had never cheated on him, and he was about to kill me for nothing. My next words were, "God, please help me." At that moment, the telephone rang, and David told me to answer it. I did, and it was his cousin Celeste asking for a cup of sugar. She didn't have any for her coffee. To me, that was God! David put the gun away and left for work. I went to work, but I was upset the entire day.

I had never told David's family or mine how mean and abusive he had been to me. Everyone thought he was such a great guy, but now I wanted them to know everything and especially that he had threatened to kill me more than once. I wanted them to know just in case he did. I didn't want my death to be an unsolved mystery. Bottom line, I was sick and tired of the way things were going between us.

The next evening, I called Celeste and asked her to come over. She said she had wanted to talk to me about Danyel. She arrived within minutes, and I was anxious to hear what she had to say. She alerted me that Danyel had mentioned to her daughter that if David hit me again, she was going to kill him. I was shocked, astonished, and totally unprepared for that reveal. My eyes filled with tears, and as I opened my mouth to speak, the words spewed out as though I was emptying my gut. When I was done, I realized I had blurted out all the abusive episodes I had been harboring within for years. I was having a meltdown, and the tears continued to flow. Celeste threw her arms around me and hugged me until I regained my composure. The effects of a hug at the right time can have a monumental impact on someone who is hurting. That hug allowed me to feel like everything was going to be all right. I thanked her for coming over, and I was glad we talked. She made sure I was okay before she left. I felt embarrassed yet relieved.

I knew I had to do something. For years, I tried to protect Danyel from the mess that was going on between her father and me. It was easy when she was a little girl, but now she was a teenager in high school, old enough to see and understand what had been happening. I never spoke against him because I didn't want her to grow to hate her father. There was no good reason for me to stay with David. I no longer trusted him. I had hoped that he would change, but there was no change in sight. He was continuing along his merry way doing his weekly thing. He seemed to be content with the life he was living. I entertained the thought that he might have been on drugs because he never had any money and wanted to fight me for mine. Lies would come out of his mouth like droplets from a sneeze. Every year, his job threw an employee Christmas party, and he always had an excuse for not taking me. He claimed he didn't want to go because they were dull and he would have a better time spending his Friday nights with his friends.

Years later, I found out he had attended them all with another woman, one of his coworkers. Ironically, one of my coworkers had attended as a guest, saw him, and came into work and asked me why I wasn't there. I never bothered to mention it to him because I didn't want to hear another lie. In my heart, I knew it was time to make a move. I just had to wait for the appropriate time.

Chapter 10

Every night, I would come home to an empty house. I had gotten used to it. I stopped going to see Danny every day after work because she was either involved in after-school extracurricular activities, softball games, or visiting friends. I was happy for her. It seemed my grandmother had softened up in her later years. I was never allowed to do those things. David continued to disappear for days at a time. I never knew when he would pop up. I learned to embrace my time alone. Sometimes, I think God wants us to be still, be quiet, and listen. I believed that God would work everything out for me in his time and in his way.

I opened my Bible and turned to the Book of Exodus. As I began to read, I was reminded how God had provided for the children of Israel in the wilderness. He went before them providing a pillar of a cloud to lead them by day and a pillar of fire to give them light by night as they traveled. He fed them with manna from heaven and supplied them with water from a rock to quench their thirst, and he protected them from the Egyptians by parting the Red Sea. I then turned to the Book of Daniel and read about Shadrach, Meshach, and Abednego, who were thrown into a fiery furnace for refusing to bow down and worship a golden image made by King Nebuchadnezzar. When the king looked into the furnace, he saw four men, three who had been bound, walking in the midst of the fire, unhurt. The fire had no power over them, and the king said the fourth was like the Son of God! Their clothes were intact, and there was no smell of fire on them. The king became a believer on that day, realizing that no other god could deliver like the God the three men served. God is with us even when we are going through the fire. He is the same yesterday, today, and forever. He has not changed. He is still performing miracles and continues to lead, provide, and protect his children.

At the age of fifteen, I was saved by God from being killed by a drunk driver while I was waiting at a bus stop. God steered the car so that it sliced my right knee, ripped off my shoe, but never knocked me down. A miracle. At the age of sixteen, after leaving a baby shower, I decided to go to my summer job and pick up my paycheck. I worked the 3:00–11:30 shift. It was my night off, and it was only a ten-minute ride away, so I walked instead of waiting on the bus. There was hardly any traffic. A car passed by me but caught my attention as it stopped, backed up, and parked. I had an uneasy feeling in my stomach. Just as I was about to pass the car, the doors opened and two men got out and walked toward me. They appeared to be middle-aged. As they approached me, I froze with fear. It felt as though my body had turned to stone. I couldn't move. One of the men asked me where I was going, and that was when I heard the voice, and it said, "Open your mouth and speak." I did open my mouth, but the words that came out were not my own. The words suggested to the two men that I was a party girl and if they had some time, they could walk with me to meet my girlfriend and we could all go out together and have some fun. The younger-looking man put his arm around me. He was all for it, but the other man said he didn't feel like walking. The voice said, "Aw, come on, you're not old, and it's not far, just up the hill." So we walked, and as we arrived, the voice said, "Wait right here while I go get her, she should be ready." They waited. As soon as I was safely inside, I collapsed. My boss immediately came to me and asked me if I was okay. All I could say was, "Two men, two men, please ask them to leave." He went out along with the chef and told them I no longer needed their services and watched as they walked away. I explained what had happened, and my boss drove me home. Years would pass before I traveled alone at night again. One thing I knew for sure, I had heard the voice of God. I had experienced another miracle.

On one other occasion, I had paid all the bills, mine and David's. His car insurance left me low on funds. I had no money for food. I had vegetables but no meat. Snow had begun to fall. The weatherman had forecast a blizzard. As I rode home, I remember thinking, "Only four more days to wait for payday." As I stepped off the trolley, I was amazed how beautiful and clean the snow looked. There were no footprints, and I felt bad that mine would be the first to mar its beauty. There were about four inches of snow on the ground. Schools and businesses had let out early for precautionary measures. I was the only one on the street. I had another block to walk when I noticed something that looked like money lying on top of the snow. Sure enough, there on top of the new fallen snow with no footprints in sight lay a ten-dollar bill, a five-dollar bill, and three one-dollar bills—eighteen dollars. I picked them up, and they were dry and warm. At the next corner, there was a grocery store. I went in and bought enough meat to last until payday and beyond. Another miracle. I then realized that God had been with me my entire life. I am so grateful for his goodness, his mercy, and his grace. He has never failed me. I will trust him for the rest of my life. I am also grateful for a mother and a grandmother who prayed for me as I was growing up. I thank God for bringing to my remembrance, through his word, that he is always with me. The Bible is not just some book you buy to enhance your library. It is to be read! I closed my Bible and settled into a peaceful night's sleep.

Chapter 11

Part 1

We've all heard the expression, "The devil is always busy." That's true. Sometimes it seems that the harder you work to build your relationship with God, the more he tries to distract you. He has a knack for glamorizing sin to make it appear as a must-have. For these reasons, we must pray without ceasing and always wear the whole armor of God as instructed in the book of Ephesians chapter 6.

I woke up from a peaceful sleep, feeling fresh and revived physically and spiritually. It was Friday, and I was excited to complete the workweek. Danny and I had planned to spend the weekend with my mother in New Jersey. I had just stepped out of the shower when I heard David downstairs. I threw on my robe as he was coming upstairs and had begun towel-drying my hair. Something was amiss. I rarely saw him between Thursday morning and Sunday evening. I immediately became apprehensive.

He came straight to the bathroom and stood in the doorway. I stood silently, waiting, not knowing what to expect as he stared at me. He began to speak in a sarcastic tone, "So you've been running your mouth, talking to my family, and now they're all on my back about you." I responded, "Yes, and every word was true. I wanted them to know. I've put up with your nonsense for seventeen years. Time after time, you've cheated on me. Time after time, you've been abusive to me. Time after time, you've lied to me, and time after time, I've forgiven you because I loved you, but guess what, time's up!" I watched his face turn red, and he had begun to swell up. Suddenly, up jumped the devil!

The scary thing about this was that the devil was me. I can't remember who grabbed who first. I think it was simultaneous. I do remember lowering my head because he always aimed for my face.

I was punching, grabbing, clawing, and writhing my body like a wild animal fighting for its life. In my mind, I was thinking, "I'll be damned if I'm going to work with a black eye today!" All of a sudden, he let go of me and stepped away. I slowly raised my head and saw blood oozing from his arms, face, and neck. He was shaking as he looked at his arms and began yelling, "Look what you've done to me!"

He said it at least three times. And I said, "Yeah, now you go to work and explain that!" He stormed out of the house. I didn't know where he went, and I didn't care. I got myself together and left for work unscathed.

Part 2

Throughout the day, my thoughts were fixed on my next move. I was wondering if I should go home or not. Supposed he came back to hurt or kill me, would he be hiding in the house planning a surprise attack? I had to think fast. My workday was almost over. Should I cancel my weekend trip with Danny and disappoint her? An idea popped into my head. I was excited to get home and execute it.

As I arrived home, I cautiously entered. Once inside, I checked all the rooms and basement to be certain no one else was there. I proceeded to the kitchen, opened the drawer beneath the countertop, and retrieved the largest, sharpest knife in the set. I took it upstairs and put it in the top drawer of my night table. *Now I am ready! If he comes in and attacks me. I am going to kill him!* I shut the drawer and came to my senses. I asked myself if that was what they meant by premeditated murder. *Why am I thinking like this? This is not who I am.* I realized I was in trouble, and I fell to my knees, looked up, lifted my hands, and cried out to the only one who could help me, "Lord, I don't want to kill anyone. Remove these thoughts from my mind. They are not from you. This problem is too big for me, please take it. I surrender, I surrender. I'm giving it to you. I'm leaving David in your hands." I cried myself to sleep. No harm came to me. Danny and I spent the weekend in Jersey. When I returned home Sunday night, David was there. He was cordial as though nothing had happened.

Chapter 12

Monday afternoon, I called Celeste to let her know that I was going to leave David. I felt it was best. She told me her family members were disappointed in David because they knew I had been good to him. She said David told them the gun wasn't loaded, that he just wanted to scare me. Well, it surely did. It scared me enough to leave him. My plan was to leave the following Monday while he was at work. I was only going to take enough clothes to last two weeks, a small television, my jewelry, and a few small personal items. He could have everything else even though all the new furnishings and appliances were bought by me. It was a small price to pay for my peace of mind. She said she understood. After I talked to her, I called my uncle, and he said he would help me move my things to my grandmother's house on Monday. I began packing and hiding my bags and suitcases in the far end of our walk-in closet.

Finally, it was Monday, and David had left for work. I called my coworker and asked if she could cover my shift. She said yes; however, she couldn't pull a double, so I had to go in and cover her shift that night. It threw a wrench in my plan, but I had no choice. I had begun gathering my belongings to take downstairs when the phone rang; it was my uncle calling to tell me he couldn't make it. Everything seemed to be going wrong. I put my things back into their hiding place. It was a wasted day. I watched a couple of talk shows and was in the process of making myself a sandwich when David came in. Immediately, I knew it was God. He had blocked my plan because he knew David would come home midday and catch me moving out. Who knows what would have happened. I thanked God.

Celeste called me and volunteered to help me move when I was ready. I prayed that night and asked God's permission to move out on Thursday. I called my coworker again, and she said she would be happy to work a double shift for me. I called Celeste and told her I would be ready Thursday morning. Wednesday night, I wrote David a four-page letter expressing all my feelings and explained why I had to leave. I wished him well. Thursday morning, I left it on the bed as I was leaving. Celeste was waiting for me. I shut the door behind me with no regrets. I had given him all I had. It was time.

Final Chapter

A day had passed before David found out I had left. He called my grandmother's asking for me, but I wasn't there the first time. Eventually, he reached me. He sounded like a desperate man. One minute he was sorrowful, and the next minute he sounded enraged. He was probably upset because now he would have to pay his own bills. He didn't ask me to come home; he demanded that I come home. I let him know that was never going to happen. There was no turning back.

Many nights I would see him sitting in his car watching me as I was leaving Bible study. I changed jobs, but I never told him because I had no idea what state of mind he was in, and I didn't want any trouble. One Sunday, he waited for me to come out of church. He called out to me and offered me a ride home so we could talk face-to-face. We had a pleasant conversation. He admitted he had been following me and was convinced that I wasn't seeing anyone else. He apologized for all the accusations and abuse. He said he now understood that God was my first love and he could not compete with him or be jealous. He asked me to promise him I would never become a religious fanatic standing on the corner talking crazy. We laughed together before parting ways, and subsequently, we became good friends. God had changed his heart, and I was so grateful and thanked God for another answered prayer. I still attended some of David's family functions, like weddings and funerals, but that was the extent of our relationship. He and Danny shared time together. As for me, I was about to step into my new life of freedom.

If the Son therefore shall make you free, ye
shall be free indeed. (John 8:36)

Danny and I shared a room at my grandmother's. She had rented out her other spare bedroom to a friend, so my priority was finding a new home for us. The room was too cluttered, and there was no air-conditioning. I didn't want an apartment, and I didn't want to move out of the city. We had already been at my grandmother's longer than I had planned. I must say we enjoyed spending time with her. I learned so many things about her I had never known. She was a very private person when it came to her personal business. She had been pregnant four times resulting in three miscarriages. Her surviving son had become a successful musician. He was a guitarist who had traveled the world until his sudden death at a young age, caused by heart disease. Soon after, she lost her husband. It was grief that brought her and my grandfather together. They never married but were good friends. She helped him raise his six children.

She had prayed her way through many personal tragedies. I admired her because she was always loving and forgiving and never bitter. I was encouraged by her wisdom and now understood why my mother entrusted me to her. She knew Ms. Anna would raise me the same way she raised her and her sisters and brothers, instilling in them the Word of God. I was glad God had positioned me to help her financially and with home repairs during our stay with her. She was a blessing to me.

I worked for a major airline and had the opportunity to travel anywhere I chose. Sometimes, I traveled with Danny, and other times alone, which was a first for me. At last, I had peace of mind and time to focus on my dream. About ten years ago, a school had closed due to budget cuts, and I thought, if I had the money, I would buy it and turn it into a community center. I knew I was really dreaming big because it would take a whole lot of money to buy a school. The building became a senior living facility; however, there was a small building next to it that had previously been some sort of annex. I thought, *Maybe someday I will be able to buy that building.*

My job required me to work the midnight shift for vacation relief. I met a very nice man named Kenneth Tyree. We became friends instantly. He was a real estate broker by day and worked for the airlines at night as a part-time mechanic. In his spare time, he liked to buy and restore old cars. He had a daughter the same age as Danny, whose name was Kenya. His wife had left them when his daughter was very young. They had prayed for years that she would come back, but tragically, she was found dead in an alley from a drug overdose. His sisters helped raise his daughter. He loved the Lord as I did, and we enjoyed each other's company. He made time to teach me how to drive, and finally, I passed my test and received my license. We talked a lot, and I shared my dream with him concerning the building, and he thought it was a great idea. We began talking to the residents in the neighborhood, and the response was amazing! Who would have guessed there were so many talented and professional people right there in the community who were willing to volunteer their time, skills, equipment, and tools, and many were willing to donate money. We met retired carpenters, seamstresses, mechanics, hairdressers, music teachers, cooks, everything we would need to serve a community. All we needed was a building.

I had heard that David was living with a young woman. They had one child together and another on the way. It didn't bother me. I just wanted him to be as happy as I was. Danny and Kenya hit it off right away. Kenneth's church sponsored a retreat at Blue Mountain, and the four of us attended. While there, the Lord laid it on my heart to write about him. That was my calling. I had been writing most of my life, but now my writings would be Christ-centered. God had restored my joy and peace. I'd made up my mind to be a traveler on a mission for the Lord.

Early one Sunday morning, I received a call from David's sister from Virginia. David had been killed in an automobile accident on his way to their family reunion. I couldn't believe the man I once called my prince was dead.

My brain went into a tailspin, searching for answers. How, why, where? Was he alone? So many questions and then a realization—I had to tell Danny, but I didn't want to do it. The next few days were exhausting from anxiety, waiting for his body to arrive, answering phone calls from concerned family and friends, having to explain over and over again, when all I wanted to do was go to sleep and wake up from this bad dream. And then came the questions about insurance. Did he have any? Who was the beneficiary? I had no idea. On Tuesday, I called his employer and Human Resources, and they confirmed that I was still his beneficiary. I was surprised because he had a new woman in his life. His family paid to have his body transported back to Philadelphia. I reimbursed them and made all the other funeral arrangements. Danny and I went to view his body at the funeral home but did not attend the services. His new family was grieving also. His two young children would grow up without their father, and their mother would have to deal with that. I knew there would be some people watching to see how the ex-wife and the other woman in his life were interacting, so I chose not to attend out of respect for her.

A year had come and gone since David's passing. His house had been left to his new family. He left me a huge sum of money. He always told me if anything ever happened to him, Danny and I would be well taken care of, and I had doubts about that because of the way things were going between us, but he kept his word. At first, I thought it was ironic that he never gave me a dime as his wife, yet he left me wealthy in his death, but after thinking about it, I knew that God was in control of the situation. David and I were not together. He had begun a new life with another family and could have changed his beneficiary, but God put it in his heart not to.

I knew that it was time to fulfill my dream. Kenneth, along with a judge and a lawyer from the neighborhood, were negotiating the legalities concerning my building. Six months later, I was presented with the deed to my dreams. I was overwhelmed by the support of the community, who were still donating. We received musical instruments, sewing machines, stage equipment, and so much more. The seniors who resided in the main building were just as eager and excited as I was to get things up and running because their knowledge and skills would be used to give them a new purpose in life. It was my desire to expose children to the arts, music, dance, theatrics, and writing. Most of these classes had been cut from the curriculum in the public schools. There are so many talented children getting into trouble because they are bored.

I had a wonderful group of people working with me. Kenneth was with me every step of the way. We were in the process of arranging and scheduling the classes. The next task was to give this building a name, and I chose to name it the David Morgan Community Center, in honor of my late husband. On the day of the dedication and grand opening, we had food, music, games, and a clothing drive. God had provided us with the most beautiful day I had ever seen, and everyone had a great time. David's daughter Sandy had come, and that was a pleasant surprise. As the tears of joy ran down my face, Kenneth turned toward me and told me he knew without a doubt that I was the woman he and Kenya had been praying for. Without further hesitation, he embraced me, kissed me, went down on one knee, and presented to me a beautiful engagement ring and asked me to marry him. I stared down into the eyes of a friend whom I had fallen in love with, and I said yes. My mind flashed back to a scripture my grandmother had given me.

> And we know that all things work together
> for good to them that love God, to them who are
> called according to His purpose. (Romans 8:28)

Twelve months later, I became Mrs. Janice Tyree. We had a big beautiful church wedding. Our daughters had come home from college to give me away. Our reception was held at the center. It had proven to be a blessing to the community, providing services and activities for the young as well as our seniors. The children had already begun rehearsals for a gospel musical, performing songs written by me. Our seniors were busy making costumes. Our musicians were practicing. All was well. Another scripture had come to mind.

> Delight thyself also in the Lord; and He
> shall give thee the desires of thine heart. (Psalm
> 37:4)

Ken sold his house, and we bought a new home together. My mother, grandmother, and the rest of my family, along with Ken's family, planned a huge housewarming celebration, and we invited the community. Other neighborhoods around the city have been watching us and are working on projects that will enhance their communities. The world is an audience. Allow them to see something beautiful in you!

Every night before bed, Ken and I thank God and ask that he would bless each and everyone, everywhere, every day. Amen.

The end.

This is my story and my song: "I'm a Traveler."

I'm a Traveler

I'm a traveler on a mission for the Lord,
I've a message from Jesus to you,
The time is near and you need to hear,
The Word of God to get you through.

I'm a witness to the power of my Savior,
I've been blessed with the goodness of his love,
From a tiny seed, I became a tree,
Proudly standing and reaching above.

Come and love the Lord as I do,
He'll make a difference in you,
There's much you can achieve, if you would believe,
That Jesus loves you too.

I'm a traveler with a message about Jesus, from the Lord,
And if you let me, I'll be a magnet drawing you closer to his Word,
I'm a traveler and my mission is you.

Now faith is the substance of things hoped
for, the evidence of things not seen.

—Hebrews 11:1

Season 4

An Appropriate Time

To everything there is a season,
And a time to every purpose
Under the heaven.

—Ecclesiastes 3:1

Seasons

The seasons of our lives are as the seasons of a year,
The only difference being, yearly seasons reappear.

At birth we enter into spring, as fresh as morning dew,
First tooth, first step, first grade, first kiss, everything's brand-new.

A first love rings in summer, as you learn the ways and hows,
Burning passion, hot desires, will lead to wedding vows.

With all debts paid and children grown, our lives are now at ease,
We take the time to look around and enjoy the autumn breeze.

The graying skies of winter match the gray upon our heads,
The firewood is burning and the quilts are on the bed.

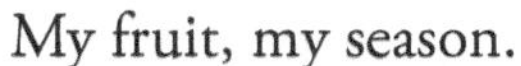

As we look about the naked trees, and see the empty nests,
We are thankful for four seasons, before the sun sets in the west.

My fruit, my season.

The Feeling

I could feel you waiting patiently, yet I ran the other way,
Prolonging the agony and the hurt, ignoring the tug at my heart that
said,
Turn around!

Sometimes I'd pick up that book, the one with the riddles and
parables
That I didn't understand,
Every now and then I thought I heard someone say, "Come!"

Then one night I prayed, trusting in that feeling that I felt coming
from you,
Asking you to pull me up out of my misery, and the voice said,
"Done!"

So then I asked, how many times must I put my trust in a feeling,
Believe and confess to a substance that I cannot see, and the voice
said, "One!"

God's Love Lifted Me

I've lived, I've laughed, I've loved,
And yet I cry, but no one knows,
I sing, I dance, I write,
And yet I hurt, but it never shows.

I've helped, I've encouraged, I've cared,
And yet I felt sad, I hid my woes,
I've given, I've fed, I've clothed,
And yet I was depressed, my spirits were low.

I began to pray in the name of Jesus,
God heard me and poured out His mercy,
He dried my tears, He removed the hurt,
He restored my hope and joy,

God's love lifted me!

Thank You

Thank you for your love that calms my fears,
Thank you for your Son, who wipes my tears,
Thank you for your words that speak to me,
Thank you for the truth that set me free,
Thank you, Lord, you taught me how to pray,
Thank you for the lamp that lights my way,
If it were not for your love,
If it were not for your Son,
If it were not for your word.
I would not be alive today!

Preserve God's Word

As I was reading God's Word, the words came to life,
and the spirit whispered in my ear,
Hold forth the word of life, that you may rejoice in the day of
Christ, fret not, I am near.

Whoso keepeth my word, in him is the love of God perfected,
Love in deed and in truth, perfect love casteth out fear,
My words shall not pass away, preserve them in your heart,
Your inheritance is reserved in heaven, be of good cheer.

For I so loved you, I sent my Son; as you have believed in him,
The promise awaits you when I shall appear,
He that hath an ear, let him hear.

I never will forget the words the spirit spoke to me.
I'm pressing on towards heaven, to life eternally.

Scriptures from the King James Bible

You're a Healer

I was sick and tired of the way things were,
I needed a shoulder to cry on,
As I prayed to your ears, you removed all my fears,
I held on to your hands,
As you helped me understand.
You're a healer, a healer of soul and mind,
You're a healer, a healer of all mankind.

I lay flat on my bed with only troubles for cover,
The blues was weighing me down,
As I remembered your words, it was your voice I heard,
I felt the warmth of your love,
It was grace from above.
You're a healer, a healer of soul and mind,
You're a healer, a healer of all mankind.

Thank you.

I'm Going to Praise You

When I was caught up in sin, you loved me when no one would,
When I was about to drown, you saved my soul as no one else could,
No matter how hard the climb or how steep the hill,
Nothing can stop me from doing your will.

When I didn't have a dime, you came and made a way,
In my darkest hours, you brightened my day,
When I was alone, you came to comfort me,
You rocked my weary soul to sleep.

I'm going to praise you every day, Lord,
You are my joy, my strength, and my peace,
I'm going to praise you every day, Lord,
For paying the price on Calvary.

Reaching for the Promise

We are reaching for the promise, trusting in the Lord,
Moving forward faithfully, towards our great reward.
Feasting in the Word of God, and praying as we go,
Obeying his instructions, rejoicing as we grow.

We are wearing God's whole armor and believing all he has said,
Through his Word we receive power, by his spirit we are led.
Confessing and repenting as we turn away from sin,
The old man has been evicted, and the new man is moving in.

We'll walk in love together as that old man peels away,
We are children of the light, and the children of the day.
Delivered from our carnal works of lust and wantonness,
Set free by our Savior, we are clothed in righteousness.

Through trials and tribulation, we will praise his holy name,
As we press our way towards the mark, we shall not be ashamed.
Preserving all God has given us, preserving all that is right,
Preserving all that is holy, marching boldly towards the light.

And when we hear from heaven, as he comes among the clouds,
Every eye shall see him, and every knee shall bow.
Triumphantly, we'll celebrate with praises from the heart,
He's King of Kings and Lord of Lords,
hallelujah! How great thou art.

Give her of the fruit of her hands; and let
her own works praise her in the gates.

—Proverbs 31:31

Bits and Pieces

Fragile is the mind that says, "Give up." It must be handled with care as though it were fine crystal, for once it breaks and shatters into bits and pieces, it no longer reflects beauty and light for all to see. Instead, it has been reduced to broken glass.

And like glass that has been swept, there may be remnants lying dormant, hidden in the crevices of the soul, tricking one's heart into believing that all is well, only to resurface when least expected, cutting, leaving scars, and thrusting the spirit into a dark place with feelings of uselessness and hopelessness.

But there is hope. Never give up! God loves you, and he can restore you. Because of him, there is a light that outshines every other light, a light that will lead you out of darkness, heal your broken heart, bind your bits and pieces, and make you whole again to shine as a witness to encourage others. His name is Jesus, the Light of the World.

Have faith, trust God, and love one another. Love can solve many of the problems in the world today.

To My Readers

It is my hope and desire that once you have read this book, you will share it with other family members and friends. This book was written to give hope and encouragement during tumultuous times, not only in our country, but in the entire world. We have all seen and experienced hard times and sadness at one time or another. We refer to them as the rainy days of life. After every great storm, God places a rainbow in the sky as a reminder that he is still in control and that all we need to do is trust him.

May this little book of mine serve as a source of light during your rainy days!

Thank you.

Patsy Long

About the Author

Patsy Long is a native of Philadelphia, Pennsylvania. As a young girl, she became an avid reader and aspired to one day become an author. Writing poems and songs for churches in her community became her passion. In later years, Patsy taught church school, and it was during that time God's spirit led her to write about him. From that day moving forward, everything she wrote was composed of words or lyrics that directed others toward him.

Writing would become a source of healing and restoration following trials she would later endure. Trials that would lead to peace and unspeakable joy. That was why she wrote this book. Patsy's life mission is to encourage others to build a relationship with God—there is nobody greater. He answers prayers and still uses ordinary people to do extraordinary things. He loved us enough to give his only begotten Son so that we may have eternal life. Trust him!